Shortcuts with Dad

Shortcuts with Dad

Tales of One Family's
Misadventures On-The-Road

Paul Siebels

Kathryn Paul

Mark Siebels

Published by Paul Siebels

In conjunction with Lulu (www.lulu.com)

Dedicated to our parents. Thanks for all the wonderful memories you provided for us during our childhood. May these memories be as enjoyable for you to read as they were for us to remember and write.

ISBN 978-0-6151-5236-3

Contents

Preface

This book is a collaborative effort between Paul, Katie and Mark. It is based on our memories of funny trips and stories that happened while we were growing up. As such, while all these stories really happened, there may be some minor inaccuracies in dates, locations, geography, and other details due to fading (and/or selective) memories. Most of the inaccuracies have been eliminated. But there may be a few left, which hopefully will not detract from the stories themselves.

Acknowledgements

Thanks to our spouses Constance, Drake, and Christina, who supported and encouraged us as we struggled for many long days and nights, trying to recall the many stories that were so much an enjoyable part of our growing up. And special thanks to Marilyn Young, who edited the book and helped eliminate the many mistakes that first time authors are prone to make. Any remaining mistakes are intentional (that's our story) and are strictly our own.

Introduction

During any one of our many family summer vacations, as we were driving down some long stretch of interstate or highway, one of us kids would invariably ask "Where are we, Dad?" "We're taking a shortcut" was the reply. "Oh, no, not another shortcut!" would come the chorus from the back seat. And so would begin another one of what became known as "Dad's Famous Shortcuts". They were never short, never what Dad expected, and they were never (well, almost never) boring. After learning that we were taking a shortcut, we would ask where we were so we could figure out how much longer it would take to get to the hotel (and the pool!). Dad's reply was often times "I don't know, but we are making good time!" So "Dad's Famous Shortcuts" followed us throughout our lives, from Camden, Maine to San Diego, California; from Alberta, Canada to Corpus Christi, Texas and everywhere in between. These shortcuts and our family vacations always seemed more like the movie, "National Lampoon's Vacation" than a Midwestern family out to see the sights. Only ours were usually funnier, because they were real life.

"Don't mind me, I'm from Iowa" was Dad's mantra when cutting across double yellow lines, making U-turns in the middle of the street and generally NOT following the rules of the road, local laws or commonly accepted road etiquette. It was repeated across many different states in many different situations in a series of family station wagons. The first vehicle that received the use of this mantra was the "Brown Bomber" as it came to be called, which was a brown, full-sized 1970 Mercury Marquis station wagon with fold up seats in the "way back". We all had our place: Dad doing the driving and Mom doing needle point in the front seat. Paul, Katie and our grandmother, if she was along, were in the back seat reading. Needless to say there was always the imaginary dividing line drawn between Paul and Katie, and if it was crossed, it started the "he's on my side" or "she's bothering me" complaints typical of kids cramped in a car. And poor little Mark suffered in the way back stuffed between six suitcases and a scotch plaid cooler filled with the "comforts" of home, (for Mom and Dad anyway). The Bomber even had a matching brown, wooden box that could be mounted on top to carry the excess suitcases on those very long trips, which made it look like a large brown turtle with its house on its back. The Brown Bomber was followed by a white, full-sized, wood-paneled 1977 Pontiac Grand Safari station wagon that Mom always referred to as the "Siebels' Bus". Her famous quote, "The Siebels' Bus is leaving!" was usually announced in a loud voice in a variety of public settings, much to the embarrassment of us kids. On very long trips, the Siebels' Bus was loaded with a seam-splitting, silver luggage bag strapped to the roof, making it look like the Beverly Hillbillies' truck with "Granny" stuck on top, wrapped in duct tape. The third family truckster was a burgundy red, full-sized (of course) 1983 Chevrolet Caprice station wagon that was occasionally referred to as the "red wagon". It carried us many miles so fully loaded in the rear that it looked like it was about to become airborne. The final oversized station wagon was a blue 1987 Buick that for some unknown reason was spared the indignity of being involved in any of the funny, embarrassing, and usually unplanned series of events that we still tell stories about at our family get-togethers. It is these stories that we have tried to capture in the following chapters.

Yellow Rose of Texas

"Family Vacation"

We went to Texas

It was very hot

My brother was a baby

My sister was not

This rhyme, recited by a girl in Paul's fifth grade class who was asked to describe her summer vacation, describes very well our trip to Texas in the spring of 1975. Paul was nine years old, Katie had just turned seven, and Mark was still three. It was a very long, hot, dry, dusty drive down to Texas from Iowa. We headed south in the spring for one of Dad's business meetings for the Maytag Company, so we were going to miss school for several days! That was the good news. The bad news was that we were going to miss so many days (two weeks), that our teachers sent HOMEWORK with us to do in the car. Yuck! How were we to have fun on vacation, if we had to do homework!?! That actually turned out to be a blessing for our parents, for whenever we started getting bored and disruptive in the back seat, they would say it was time to do two or three more pages of homework. That usually quieted things down to a low grumble for the next hour or two.

For the trip down, we were all packed into the Brown Bomber. Dad's brown wooden box, strapped to the top of the car, was loaded with suitcases. Even with that added space, the back end of the Bomber was filled to the ceiling. The three of us had to cram into the back seat with all of our toys and books (and homework) to last us for the trip. Clark Griswold had nothing on us.

Just like the scene in "Family Vacation" where the Griswold's stop at the Grand Canyon, jump out of the car, run up to the rim of the canyon and snap a picture, then jump back into the car and drive off, Dad would do the same. He always had his camera on trips and was always stopping somewhere, so he could "just jump out and take a picture"! On this trip, early one morning as we were driving somewhere in Texas, Dad spied a big Prickly Pear cactus along side of the highway. He quickly pulled over, and ordered all of us kids out of the car to go stand by the cactus to have our picture taken. Katie kept worrying that she was going to get stuck by the cactus, Mark kept bending over to pick up rocks and bugs and plants, and Paul kept having his cowboy hat blown off by the wind. But eventually Dad got the picture he wanted, and we all jumped back in the car and drove off. The Family Vacation was under way again!

"Do You Have a License For That?"

The trip to Texas took place right in the middle of the first "oil crisis", when gas jumped from 60-70 cents per gallon to over $1 a gallon! And for a brief time, there was even gas rationing. As Murphy's Law would have it, the rationing was still going on during our trip. The rule for the rationing system was that people who had a license plate that ended in an even number could get gas on even numbered days of the month, while those with an odd number could get gas on the odd numbered days. This could have been a problem for us, since we were traveling long distances almost every day, at least at the beginning and end of the trip. Not wanting to be caught short during the trip, Dad came up with a "creative" solution. At that time, we had not only the Brown Bomber, but also an old, green Buick Le Sabre that had been given to our parents by our grandmother. Dad had just renewed both vehicle licenses not too long before, at the same time, so their license plates were in numerical sequence, which meant that one was odd and the other even. His solution was to take the license plate from the green Buick with us on the trip so he would have both an odd numbered and even numbered plate, as needed on any particular day. As a result, there were those times during the trip where first thing in the morning, usually while it was still dark, Dad would go out to the car with his screw driver and change the license plate on the back of the car (Iowa didn't require a front plate at that time). Had a policeman or sheriff driven by right then, he might have had a lot of explaining to do. But fortunately, we got through the trip without any embarrassing questions about our license plate.

"Cash or Credit?"

It is a fact of life that Americans charge almost everything to their credit card. Our family was no exception, especially when we traveled. Dad paid for the hotels, sightseeing, gas, souvenirs, and almost everything on a credit card, and he usually had several (in case one got maxed out). Mom did carry cash during the trip, which was usually used to pay for our meals and little treats we would get as we drove along. One of Dad's famous sayings was "I'll pay you back", whenever he would ask Mom to borrow money to pay for something. But most of the time he used his credit card. Normally this wasn't a problem, but during our trip through Texas, at one little gas station in the middle of nowhere, it could have been.

We had been driving most of the morning, and finally had pulled off the interstate to stop and stretch, use the rest rooms, and get gas. It was a small Shell gas station, located near a very small Texas town that just happened to be located on the interstate. We all got out and waited in line to use the single rest room on the side of the gas station while Dad filled up the Brown Bomber. As we came back and were standing around, Dad finished filling the tank and got out his wallet to pay for the gas. The station attendant had come out, a little old man, with dark, wrinkled skin, weathered by the sun and wind, to collect the payment. Dad pulled out his Shell credit card and handed it to the attendant. Well, they must not use many credit cards in that part of Texas, because the poor attendant looked at the card for awhile, then turned it over and looked at the back of the card for an equally long time, then turned it back over and looked at the front again. After what seemed forever, he finally ambled off to the office and was gone for quite a while. We were beginning to wonder whether he was calling the police to come get us, or the Shell Company to figure out what to do with the card. Finally he came back with the card and the appropriate receipt for Dad to sign. After he signed and got his copy, we all quickly got back into the car and headed off before the man changed his mind. We never learned why the man was so interested in, or perplexed by, the credit card, but since no one came looking for us, we figured it must have been all right.

"It *is* called Bubblegum"

It is said that "In Corpus Christi you will find smooth sea breezes and endless blue skies year-round. ...it offers guests an exciting opportunity to experience a rich blend of culture in the relaxed atmosphere of this historic coastal port." That may be well and good, but as a kid from the Midwest, all you care about is the beach. So Dad, being the considerate Dad that he was, had booked a wonderful hotel right on the beach, and his children couldn't have been happier.

The first day was spent on the beach with all the sand castle building, wave surfing and beach action a young child could stand. That is until Mark, recently introduced to the joys of bubblegum bubble-blowing, wanted to show everybody his new talent. Being the youngest of three children and always feeling like he needed to prove himself, he decided this bubble could not be ordinary; this bubble had to be the coup de grace of a young boy's skill in the art of bubble blowing. So with all his might he blew a bubble, and blew, and blew with the excitement of any young boy showing off for his Mom, Dad, big brother, sister and Nanny. (Our grandmother was affectionately known as "Nanny" because when Paul was a young toddler, he couldn't pronounce "Granny", which is what she wanted to be called. Instead it came out as "Nanny" and the name stuck.) He blew a bubble that grew to the size of a Rhode Island. Ok, maybe not that big, but for him it seemed to be quite a bit bigger than his own head. Now, being so young and new to the physics of the gum bubble, Mark didn't realize that the beach was probably not the best place to be blowing a world-record-breaking bubble. A swift wind blew up and popped that wonderful bubble, and then swirled the remnant around to where it almost fully encased Mark's head. Poor Nanny had the joy of trying to extract Mark from his mask of pink sticky gum. The rest of the day and probably the rest of the trip was spent dabbing, scraping, freezing, blotting, picking, peeling and only somewhat successfully removing the bubble gum.

"Bottoms Up"

During our stay at Corpus Christi for Dad's business meeting and our vacation, the days were filled with sightseeing, playing on the beach, and swimming in the hotel pool. One hot day we were at the pool as usual. Dad was out with us, since it was the week after his meeting so by then he really was on vacation. In those days, hotel pools still had diving boards, and Dad would entertain us with his "fancy" diving and his canon ball splashes. We would laugh and cheer and rate how big of a splash he would make with his canon balls or how good his dives were. One particular dive, Dad went a little too deep, and on the way up skinned both of his knees on the bottom of the cement pool. That ended his diving show. He spent the rest of the morning sitting on a chair with his feet up on a footstool and a wet towel over his skinned knees to ease the pain, watching us play and jump and dive. Shortly after his mishap, a young, attractive woman in a bikini started to jump and dive off the diving board. Not to say she was trying to show Dad up, but she proved to be a pretty good diver. Dad glanced at her occasionally (wink, wink), as he was nursing his knees. At one point, as she climbed up the ladder in front of us to get out of the pool, Dad asked her if she was having any problems with the bottom. She gave him a very hard look, and then, as she adjusted her bikini, said no, but she was having problems with the top. We all hooted and howled with laughter as Dad's jaw dropped and he turned bright(er) red. He then stammered no, he meant the bottom of the pool, as he uncovered his bloody knees and pointed to them. Needless to say we laughed even more as we later told Mom what had happened. Her comment was that it served him right.

Hawaiian Beach Parties

"Road to Hana"

Some people consider Lombard Street in San Francisco the most crooked street in the world, but we found a road that was much worse, in more ways than one. It happened while we were vacationing in Hawaii in 1977. This trip included time visiting our relatives who lived on the island of Maui. One day they suggested we go visit the scenic town of Hana, on the far side of the island. It was in a fairly secluded area, but they said it is very beautiful, and well worth the trip. We agreed, and all got ready to go exploring. We had already spent many days at the beach both on Maui and the big island of Hawaii, so we were ready for something different. We got that, and a whole lot more. Red and Mary warned us that the road to Hana was a rustic road, but Dad was sure we would have no problem. So off we went in our rental car - a small station wagon, of course. We headed east along the highway, following their directions to get to Hana. As we got farther along, the traffic became more and more sparse. The highway got narrower and narrower, going from a four lane road in the main city of Kahului, to two lanes outside of town, headed toward the east coast of the island. This side of the island was dominated by, and a product of, the great volcano "Haleakala"; still active, though quiet in recent years. As we reached the halfway point of the 52 mile drive to Hana, and started to head south down the eastern side of the island, closest to the volcano, the road narrowed even further. It transformed into an old, single, worn lane that wound in and around the folds of the lava flows as they spilled down from the volcano's 10,000 foot summit all the way to the sea. The road was barely wider than the car, with only a couple of feet to spare. Then it dropped hundreds of feet straight down a rocky cliff to the ocean crashing against the rocks below. The other side of the road rose straight up a jagged, bare rock face as far as the eye could see. The road wound around more than 600 curves and 50 one-lane bridges, through tropical forests with scattered waterfalls splashing down beside and then under the road. Only a few dozen feet of the road were usually visible ahead before it disappeared around another curve. When we met another car coming from the other direction, we often had to stop and back up to a wide spot in the road in order to have room enough to pass. Even then, Dad would have to move the car over so close to the rocks that the bushes would scratch the side of the car, while the people in the car passing us would be peering wide-eyed down the other side, looking straight down the cliffs and hoping that they wouldn't slip off. The trip was very quiet as we held our breath while squeezing past another car. At the same time, we were constantly struck speechless by the beauty of a sudden burst of colorful flowers in a bright patch of sun next to a bubbling stream, flowing rapidly down the mountain. By the time we reached Hana, over 3 hours from the time we left Kahului, we were convinced that the road to Hana was the most beautiful, and most difficult, road that we had ever traveled on.

"My little Hukilau"

Hawaii is a special place and as kids we were lucky enough to visit there twice. Well, most of us anyway. After our initial Hawaii trip in 1977, Mom and Dad liked it so much that they knew they wanted to go back. That time came in the summer of 1989 as a "graduation present" for Mark and Katie. Poor Paul was already married and didn't join us for this trip (though he and his wife Constance did get to go to Hawaii later that year on their own as a "first year anniversary" present from Mom and Dad).

One of the highlights of the trip was a sunset cruise more commonly known as a booze cruise on the Kiele V, a huge 55 foot catamaran. It was a wonderful trip. Katie and Mark ran around loving the boat and its impressive size. Mom and Dad wondered at the views and enjoyed the free drinks. After the cruise was over it was time for dinner. We went to a local eatery called Wiki Wiki Pizza and Deli, and while there Dad had a couple more beers (which is another story in itself). Katie and Mark were no longer young children, and Mom and Dad had enjoyed this fact throughout our trip. Not only could we explore on our own, have some of our own money, and drive the rental car, but we were old enough to "understand" that adults sometimes liked to partake in adult beverages. Looking back now this may have been one of the deciding factors for us to take the sunset cruise. Of course Mom and Dad wanted to get their money's worth and had enjoyed themselves thoroughly throughout the ride. Since Mark was designated to drive everyone back to the hotel after dinner, for obvious reasons, this was not a problem. However, as we were about to find out, the day's intake of alcohol had reached a point that Dad felt like he had been hit by Cupid's arrow.

Part of the local culture we learned about on the trip was the Hukilau, which is a Hawaiian song accompanying a hula dance that celebrates a festival that honors fishing. We had seen it performed at a luau and heard the song a number of times so it was familiar to us. Dad, however, either forgot what it was, didn't know what it was, or didn't care. As Mark was driving back to the hotel, Dad was in the back seat snuggling up to Mom, saying over and over "you're my little Hukilau". She, of course, was having none of it. Dad was laughing and giggling and Mom was rolling her eyes! When we reached the hotel, Mark dropped everyone else at the door and went to park the car. Mom, Dad and Katie went up in the elevator, and after they got off on their floor, Dad slumped down on a bench in the hall, saying he needed to "rest". When Mark made it back to the room, he announced that Dad was asleep on the bench in the hall, to which Mom replied, "We know, just leave him there." Dad did finally make it back to the room, but ended up falling asleep in his Hawaiian print swim suit and matching shirt on top of the bed. He didn't even bother taking his shoes off, getting under the blankets or even picking his feet off the floor! So much for his "little Hukilau"!

"The Long Awaited Pizza"

Everyone loves pizza. The Siebels family is no exception. We didn't get to have it very often however, and when we did it was usually on vacation. However, these simple, casual dinners always seemed to be an adventure for us.

One of our first nights in Hawaii in 1989 we went out to a local pizza place. We had been waiting forever to get our pizza, when our waiter finally admitted they had dropped it on the floor and had to re-make it. Dad wanted another beer, but he wasn't going to pay for it since it was the restaurant's fault it was taking so long. There ended up being a big scene with Dad yelling at the manager while Mom, Mark and Katie tried to make themselves invisible. The situation only got worse when we left the restaurant. Mark and Katie had gone out to get the car while Dad haggled with the manager and paid the bill. But when we got to the car, it wouldn't start! Katie refused to re-enter the restaurant on the grounds of extreme embarrassment, so it fell to Mark to go back in and inform Dad of our predicament. After ranting and raving at the entire restaurant, Dad had to, very sheepishly, ask to use the phone to call the car rental company. We were all embarrassed at that point, and ended up waiting outside for them to bring another car. We would never forget waiting for our pizza or waiting for our car and the restaurant managers probably never forgot it either.

"Honky Tonk Pizza"

Another great pizza adventure took place in Memphis when Dad and Mark had gone to a local pizza place to pick one up and take it back to the hotel. When they walked into the pizza place/bar, the first thing they noticed was that they were the only Caucasian people there. Not wanting to turn around and walk out, Dad confidently went up to the bar and placed the order for the pizza and some drinks since he and Mark were going to wait there for it. After paying for the order, they took their drinks and sat down at a table. After a few minutes, Dad got a startled look on his face and said, "They didn't take my name! How are they going to know which order is ours?" Mark calmly sipped his soda and said, "Dad, he probably just wrote 'honky' on the ticket!"

"Let it Slide"

The final pizza adventure occurred in Virginia when Dad and Mark once again went out to get a pizza and bring it back to the hotel. Everyone was starving! For some mysterious reason, unknown even to Dad, when they returned, Dad walked into the room carrying the pizza tucked up under his arm like a newspaper! Katie yelled, "Dad!" in that accusing, whiny voice teenagers use on their parents when they think they have done something embarrassing or stupid. Everyone was mortified! Dad had no idea why he was carrying it that way. Everyone knows you have to carry a pizza box flat! It was a pretty sorry looking pizza. All the cheese and toppings had slid off to one side. Mom used a plastic fork and tried to spread everything out again, but it was basically a lost cause. It was edible, though, and we were hungry! We didn't let Dad live that down for a very long time!!

"Lessons Learned"

Mark got a valuable lesson in marketing while in Hawaii. As with any vacation destination everything costs money. Taking a trip with the family from Iowa to Hawaii is no small feat in itself and thus we did not have tons of money to spend on extra-curricular activities while on vacation. Mom and Dad however, did a wonderful job of saving money at home, (by making the kids eat hot dogs wrapped in white bread, for example) so on trips we could really do almost everything we wanted to. Although Mom had started making her own money creating stained glass art which gave us more freedom while on this trip to Hawaii than maybe some of our previous trips, we still needed to be conscious of our budget.

Mark was just out of high school and would have done anything and everything that was wild if he thought he could get away with it. Knowing he couldn't, he thought he'd found the perfect solution when the hotel they were staying at offered FREE scuba diving lessons. He went running up to Mom asking her if he could do it and explained that it was free, so there was no problem. Mom, understanding the ways of the world, reluctantly agreed and wondered where the catch was. The lessons were great – the class met at the hotel pool, the hotel provided all the equipment, and everyone got suited up and dove in. The lesson lasted about 45 minutes and by the end of it even the newlywed who could not swim was enjoying herself.

The most important lesson had yet to be learned. After the class had concluded and all the students were thoroughly enthralled with scuba diving, especially Mark, the teacher announced that he was taking the class to the ocean (we were on the beach in Hawaii after all.) The next thing you know, Mark is once again running up to Mom asking if he can go scuba diving in the ocean with the rest of his class. Then the final lesson was learned when he had to explain to her that to go out into the ocean was going to cost $50. This is actually not a bad price, but for FREE scuba diving, it was quite a shock for

Mark. He did get to go and had a wonderful time, feeding the fish, and watching the cliff divers from the bottom looking up. But this lesson on the old bait-and-hook scheme, or whatever you want to call it, has lasted as long as the wonderful memories of scuba diving. Here endith the lesson.

New England Clam Chowder

"Camping in Camden"

On most of our family vacation trips, we stayed in a Holiday Inn, Ramada Inn, or some other similar mid-budget hotel, as long as it had a pool or was near a beach. We had stayed at many of them all over the US, from Boston to San Diego. They were comfortable, consistent, and clean. And did we mention they had a pool!? Occasionally, we got to stay at a nicer hotel, especially if Nanny was with us (paying the hotel bill!) or if Dad's business meeting was at a big convention center. But one thing we never did was camp out. Mom and Dad were just not the camping types. Dad's idea of roughing it was not having a TV. Mom's idea of roughing it was not having a restaurant in the hotel. So most of the time, we stayed in modest but nice hotels with all the amenities. But on our New England trip in 1978, Dad decided to try something a little different, as a treat, that came as close to camping as we had ever been.

The New England trip was going to be a long one, covering a lengthy drive through eastern Canada, then coming down through Maine, Vermont, New Hampshire, and Massachusetts. This was capped off with the interminable drive back to Iowa. Because of all this, Dad decided to look for at least one place to stay that would be a little different. When it came time to make hotel reservations, he checked out several different places along the route, and in Camden, Maine, he found something very different.

As we drove down from Canada, Dad told us that we were going to have a neat place to stay in Camden. Now to us kids, "neat" meant that the hotel had a pool, beach, or both. Dad assured us that this special place had both a beach and a pool. By then we were really looking forward to this stop. Mom and Dad were looking forward to it as well, because the inn where we would be staying had individual cottages for rooms, and Dad had reserved two of them: one for us kids, and one for just him and Mom! The farther south we went, the greater the anticipation! As we arrived at the inn, we were greeted by an old, rambling, white house with a huge lawn sloping down to the ocean. Several small white cottages lined up like soldiers along one edge of this enormous expanse of grass. On the opposite side was a small, outdoor pool. We were excited because we got to sleep by ourselves, with our "own" beach and a pool! What more could any kid want? As it turned out, quite a bit more. After Dad checked in and got the keys to the cottages, we grabbed our suitcases and headed for our "rooms". Approaching our cottage, we opened the door and surveyed our domain. What we kids found was a nice little room with three beds and a bathroom, and no parents. This was going to be great. Mom and Dad went to their cottage and opened their door. What they found was a nice little room with two <u>single</u> beds and a bathroom, and no TV or air conditioning. This was going to be "interesting", as Mom said. The first thing we did after dropping off our luggage was to check out the pool. It was small and unheated, with a cement sidewalk and chain link fence around it that had seen better days. Hmmm. Maybe we would spend most of our time down on the beach instead. As soon as we got permission, we headed down the hill, eager to play on the beach. When we got there, what we found was a small, sandy strip at the bottom of a short bluff. Old, rickety wooden steps led down to it, and once we stepped off at the bottom, the beach seemed to have more rocks than sand. Despite being the hot, muggy days of July, the water was very cold. We certainly wouldn't be doing much swimming or sunbathing down there. This was going to be a little bit rougher than all of us had imagined. As it turned out though, it still was a lot of fun. We were, after all, sleeping all by ourselves (which meant Mom and Dad wouldn't be telling us to stop jumping on the beds, or that it was time to be quiet and go to sleep.) And we could go walking on the beach, collecting rocks and other interesting things washed up by the waves. For Mom and Dad, they were sleeping by themselves without the family chaos that always happens while traveling. Even if they were sleeping a little bit more by themselves than they had hoped. We all had a good time visiting the little shops in Camden, seeing the harbor, and all the other things that make Maine a lot different from the Midwest. But we all agreed that as far as luxury accommodations go, the Camden cottages were a lot closer to a rough campout than to the Ritz-Carlton.

"Catch Me If You Can"

In the wintertime, Stowe, Vermont is a premier destination for skiers in the Northeast. But it has a lot of fun activities in the summertime as well. During our New England trip, Dad took us to one of those great attractions, known as the Alpine Slide. The Alpine Slide was a 2300 foot long, twisting, curving, concrete track that wound its way down the mountain, on which the adventurous could ride down on a wheeled toboggan. The toboggan even came equipped with a hand brake, so the timid could control their speed during their descent. At the time, Paul was 14, Katie was 11, and Mark was 8. Dad figured Paul would have no problem with the ride, and Mark was gung ho to go down, since he was at the age where he thought he could do anything. But Katie was a little scared and wasn't sure she wanted to go down at all. Mom said no way would she risk a bad case of road rash. In the end, Paul took the lead, followed by Mark (who didn't want to follow Katie, because he wanted to go fast and was sure she would slow him down). Then it was Katie's turn, with Dad right behind her to encourage and help her if necessary. Once that was decided, everyone was all set. Paul took off riding down the track at moderate speed. Mark followed, and both were quickly out of sight. Katie carefully climbed on board her toboggan, with Dad coaching her on how to use the hand brake, as she prepared to take off. Dad then gave her a gentle push, and she slowly started rolling down the track, headed for the first curve a few yards down the hill. Dad got his toboggan set up, and pushed off as Katie disappeared around the first curve. As Dad picked up speed he applied the brake so he wouldn't run into Katie when he caught up with her. But as he came out of the curve, Katie was already disappearing around the next one. Dad eased up on the brake and allowed his toboggan to pick up speed. Going faster and faster, he kept expecting to catch up to Katie just ahead. But each time he rounded a curve, there was no sign of her. He began scanning the sides of the track to make sure that she hadn't had a spill and fallen off. Soon he was zooming down the track, braking just enough to prevent himself from flying off the track. By the time he reached the bottom, he was worn out from all his effort to catch up to Katie. As he rolled to a stop at the finish line, Katie was already standing at the entrance gate, jumping up and down, asking "can we do that again!?" Mom asked what happened, and all Dad could say was he started Katie off and then he never saw her again. The funny part was that Mark, who was so gung ho, turned out to be the one who was a little scared and constantly used the hand brake. Katie had quickly caught up to him and kept urging him to go faster! We were all disappointed when we couldn't take the time to go down the slide again, if only to outdo Katie's wild ride!

"Keystone Comedy"

Whenever we were on a vacation that included a business trip for Dad, Mom would take us sightseeing while Dad was in his meetings. On our New England trip, while staying in Vermont, we visited the Shelburne Museum, just down the road from Burlington. This museum is filled with old homes, stores, buildings, and other artifacts from the late 1800s. One of the more interesting sights was the Ticonderoga, an old steamer that was used for day excursions on Lake Champlain, serving ports along the New York and Vermont shores. It was carefully maintained and beautifully outfitted. There were also old school buildings, a light house, a steam engine, and a covered bridge, just to name a few. We spent the day there and had a great time looking at all the historic sites, especially the steamship. Needless to say, when we saw Dad that night, we enthusiastically related to him the great day we had and all of the wonderful sights we saw, including the Ticonderoga. After a long, hard day of meetings, Dad was probably just a little bit envious of the fun we had had. But as usual on our combined vacations/business trips, he had planned some extra time in the area after his business meeting ended so that he could be on vacation as well. He decided that he would go spend some time at the museum so he could take a few pictures. Since we had all been there and didn't especially want to spend another day there, we simply dropped Dad off at the museum while we went shopping or swimming, planning to pick him up at the main entrance that evening before it closed. When we arrived later in the day and sat waiting for him at the entrance, a security guard came up and told Mom that she couldn't park at the entrance, she needed to go down to the parking lot. Despite her protestations, he insisted we had to go, so we left. Unbeknownst to us, Dad at that moment was walking towards us, and saw us as we drove off. He quickly followed us on foot. Unfortunately, the parking lot was quite a distance from the main entrance. Once we arrived there, we sat for a few minutes, and then Mom decided to drive back around to the main entrance to see if Dad was waiting there. To make matters worse, the parking lot was on a one way road that wound through the museum grounds, so we had to leave by a different exit, drive down the main highway, and come back through the main entrance. Once again, we drove off, just as Dad appeared on the scene and saw us leave. He yelled and waved, to no avail, as we disappeared out of the exit gate. As we drove back to the main entrance, Dad ran back there as well taking a direct route through the museum displays to try to get there quicker. Even with his shortcut, we arrived back at the entrance long before Dad did. We waited a couple more minutes, before Mom got worried that maybe Dad had gone to the parking lot. So off we went again, back to the parking lot, following the same winding road. Once again, Dad arrived on the scene just as our tail-lights disappeared down the road. By this time, the security guard had noticed our little episode (and probably also noticed Dad, struggling and out of breath), so he offered to drive Dad in his golf cart down to the parking lot to catch up with us. Dad gladly accepted, as by this time he was not only hot and tired, but hot under the collar as well! As they neared the parking lot, Dad saw Mom looking around, and got worried that she was about to drive off again. So he pointed at our car and loudly told the security guard, "If that car moves again, hit it!" But the guard didn't have to do that, fortunately. Once we found out what had happened, it was a very quiet ride back to the hotel with Mom apologizing over and over again. It was a long, long time before we could all laugh at that story together.

"The City Bus"

Dad would often use his mantra "don't mind me, I'm from Iowa", when confronted with an unexpected situation that required creative driving. In some cases, however, this led to surprising and sometimes hair-raising, results. During our New England trip, we were in Boston for a few days. Driving in a really big city was a new experience for us kids. Dad, however, was a pro at it. But even he was occasionally frustrated, as was the case in Boston. We were approaching the city, with our hotel destination firmly in mind, though not firmly on the map. For us kids, it meant another swimming pool. For Mom and Dad, it meant the "comforts" from home sitting in the scotch plaid-colored cooler. But getting there was proving to be a bit of a challenge. Dad was sure he knew how to get to the hotel, but we weren't getting any closer, and all the one way streets and narrow roads that twisted and turned everywhere did not help. At one point, Dad realized he had turned down the wrong street, so he decided to do a U-turn in the middle of the street. As he executed his turn, the Siebels' Bus (our white Pontiac station wagon) showed one of its shortcomings

- it had a wide turning radius. We only got half way around, and were now sitting broadside to traffic. As it happened, a Boston city bus had just turned the corner and was headed down the street towards us. Now being from the Midwest, we all expected the bus to slow down and wait for us to get out of the way. But that is not how it is done out East. The big city bus kept bearing down on us, picking up speed as it came. Dad continued to back up and tried to finish turning around as fast as he could but the bus kept getting closer and closer and our eyes kept getting bigger and bigger. When we finally straightened out and started back down the street, the bus came roaring by, coming within inches of our car, as it barreled past. We weren't sure whether this was normal big city driving or not, and we weren't sure if Dad knew what he was doing, or if we were plain lucky. But we were all glad to get to the hotel that day.

"By All Means"

Traveling with Nanny always made a unique trip, and was usually an adventure. It made the trip a little more cramped in the car, with six people instead of five, and usually an extra suitcase or two. But that was usually compensated for at the hotel because we had two rooms instead of just one. There were other aspects of the trip that were different when Nanny came along as well. Since Nanny had been a school teacher, she still tended to correct our grammar when we were talking. She was always reminding us to mind our manners at the table when we were eating, no matter whether we were having a formal dinner at a five star restaurant, or a five minute grab and go at McDonalds. And it was not only us kids who had to watch our behavior. Mom and Dad had to watch what they were saying and doing as well. For example, while Nanny didn't mind Mom and Dad bringing the "comforts of home" along in the scotch plaid cooler, she usually frowned if she thought they were getting too comfortable, even after a long day's drive. But one time she surprised us all.

We were headed to Provincetown at the tip of Cape Cod after leaving Boston on our New England trip. Nanny had been there the previous fall and kept talking about the darling cottages with their miniature gardens and white picket fences and the colorful trees. Unfortunately, they were on a two-lane highway, not the main interstate. Nanny was so excited about showing them to us that she insisted Dad take the scenic route so we could see them. It became painfully obvious shortly after we got on the two-lane road on a Friday morning at the height of tourist season was that all Dad was going to see were red tail lights and back bumpers as traffic slowed to a crawl. Nanny's conversation describing what we were going to see got quieter and quieter. Dad said nothing, but just looked grim as he stared at the miles of backed up traffic. As his visage became darker, Mom got more and more nervous and everyone else got more and more quiet, especially Nanny. She knew she had made a mistake having Dad come this way.

All of a sudden, Dad pulled off the road into a restaurant parking lot announcing, "No McDonald's today. I want to eat here." Needless of say, he got no argument from anyone, least of all Nanny. It was a darling restaurant (Mom's description) on a little bay with patio dining out by the water. When we sat down the waitress asked what we wanted to drink. No one minded when Dad ordered a Bloody Mary. As we studied the menu and sipped our drinks, everyone began to relax a bit. After a while, the waitress came by again and asked Dad if he wanted another Bloody Mary. Nanny, who normally frowned on more than one drink at noon, especially when driving, immediately piped up, "By all means!" We were all surprised at Nanny's response, but quickly nodded our agreement. Dad finally got over his bad mood with the second drink and a good lunch. It was probably that second Bloody Mary making Dad just a bit mellow that led to us acquiring the eagle....

"The Eagle Has Landed"

As many family vacationers do, we always tried to find little souvenirs or other items to take home with us to remind us of the places we had been. For us kids, it was usually a toy or trinket with the name of a park or museum stamped on it. For Mom and Dad, it was often a black and white ink print of a local landmark or scenic area. Occasionally, though, Mom and Dad decided to bring home something a little more unique and representative of the trip. Or at least Mom decided, and Dad agreed. That was what had happened during our New England trip.

While driving around the many scenic towns in Vermont, New Hampshire, and Massachusetts, Mom and Dad had admired the many different styles of architecture and decorating that they saw in the elegant old homes. For them, it was an exciting change from all the plain, ordinary houses that were all over the Midwest. For us kids, it was just something to be endured between our opportunities to go swimming in the various hotel pools. However, we knew better than to say anything, because if we started acting up or complaining, we would lose our swimming privileges for the day. And that was a fate far worse than sightseeing! So we usually read our books or played games as Dad drove around, with the occasional mumbled agreement about some nice home or sight that Mom and Dad pointed out. One feature that particularly appealed to Mom was the various entrance decorations that were placed above the doorways to many homes. She thought they added a nice touch of individuality. She was especially taken with the many plaques and sculptures of eagles that were mounted on many homes. Mom decided that she wanted to find an eagle to take home and put above the doorway of our new home on 18th Street. As a result, at every souvenir and gift shop that we went in, Mom checked out the various eagles that they had available. As fate would have it, there was a gift shop or souvenir shop or nautical shop on every street corner, usually two or three in a row. Time after time when we were out sightseeing, Mom would have Dad pull in to a parking lot and we would all wander in to a shop to browse around while Mom scouted for eagles. Unfortunately, our house had one major difference from the houses out in New England. We had a large portico over our front entranceway, which had a very wide, open space for mounting any type of object. In New England, most houses had a very small space over the entranceway due to the many windows, gables, and other architectural features common to the region. As a result, the many eagles and other decorations that Mom found that could be mounted above a door were relatively small, about a foot in width, and would look lost on the ten foot wide space above our doorway. Mom was getting more and more discouraged, Dad was getting more and more frustrated, and we kids were getting more and more bored as the days went on. Dad even got to the point where he said he wasn't going to stop any more unless Mom actually saw one she wanted. That pretty much meant that we weren't going to get one, which made her very disappointed. But Mom could tell when Dad had been pushed to his limit, so she didn't say anything more. She just kept watch out the window as we drove through the small towns or down the country lanes lined with antique shops.

She was still watching as we continued our drive out to Provincetown on the two-lane highway after our lunch stop. We kids were busy with our books while Nanny watched for pretty cottages and Dad concentrated on the traffic. But all of us practically jumped out of our seats when Mom suddenly shouted "There's one!" Dad almost hit the rear end of the car in front of him. "There's one what?!" he wanted to know. "A big eagle!" "Are you sure it's big enough for you?" he asked skeptically. "Yes, it's huge!" "Where?" he wanted to know. Mom became a bit more reserved. "On the outside wall of that gift shop back there." During this conversation, of course, we had continued driving down the road. Dad was not known for turning around for anything, and it was very rare that he did. In fact, many of his famous "shortcuts" were the result of not wanting to go back the same way we came. Now, however, for the first time in anyone's memory, he actually turned the car around and went back. Mom was blessing that second Bloody Mary! It was awfully quiet in the car for the next few minutes as we drove back to the gift shop Mom pointed to. But there, on the side of the shop, was a three-foot-wide, black, wrought-iron eagle. Even Dad had to grudgingly admit that it was a big eagle. So Mom ecstatically went in and bought the eagle. While they were wrapping up her purchase, the two little white-haired ladies who apparently owned the shop peered out the window at the over-loaded station wagon, and wondered aloud, "Where are they going to put it!?" Dad had to carefully rearrange the suitcases in the back of the station wagon to make enough room to slide the eagle in on top of them. Many miles and many days later, Dad carefully mounted Mom's eagle on the front of the house. The eagle had landed.

We're Not in Kansas Anymore

"Museum Malaria"

Many of the Siebels' vacations were in states and locations far away from the "homestead" in central Iowa, but a few were closer to home. There was a winter retreat to Lake Lawn Lodge at Delavan, Wisconsin. There were spring field trips to historic places in Illinois, like the lead mines of Galesburg and the Abraham Lincoln home in Springfield. And there were even several lazy summer weeks spent at a friend's cabin in northern Iowa. But the highlight of vacation spots in the Midwest was a trip to Chicago - if your definition of "highlight" was a large city with more people and museums than you could shake a stick at. And for one particular member of the Siebels' clan, it was not.

We had gone to Chicago one spring back in the 1970's, in order to see the big city sights. For kids from a small town in Iowa, it was new, exciting, and BIG. And Dad took us all to see the more important places. One of the most interesting for Paul and Mark was the Museum of Science and Industry. It had all kinds of neat exhibits that young boys could climb on, look into, and play with. There was even a giant glass ball that when you touched it, fiery bolts of electricity would shoot from a center point to the outer glass wherever it was touched. As exciting as it was for the boys, it was just okay for Katie. She just wasn't in to the types of exhibits that interested Paul and Mark, though there was enough there that kept her interest, at least for awhile. Next was the Field Museum, with all of its animal, mineral and historical displays. Once again, Paul and Mark enjoyed all the displays, including the many nature dioramas. But Katie was partly scared, partly bored, partly disgusted (especially looking at the reptiles.) Everyone enjoyed the Shedd Aquarium, even Katie, although she was more interested in the dolphins and other sea mammals than the fish or sharks. It was fun to watch the various shows, and even more fun to walk by all the huge fish tanks, taller than Dad was. We were surrounded by swimming fish. Another interesting place we visited was the Adler Planetarium, with its star display and informative shows. By the time we had walked around and saw all the sights in all of these museums and the aquarium, we were all getting a little tired. Dad, however, had not run out of things he wanted to see. Being the caring father that he was, when we had stopped for a break, he did ask our opinion about whether we wanted to go on to the Chicago Art Museum. Katie didn't waste a second with her answer, "If you take me to another museum, I'm going to throw up!" With that, Dad decided that we had had enough for the day and that it was time to head back to our hotel before Katie had a case of museum sickness.

"Little Black Cloud"

Most of the Siebels' vacations occurred during the summer. And it always seemed hot, humid, and not very much breeze, no matter where we ended up. But that just meant that it was perfect for playing in the pool, at the lake, or on the beach somewhere! There were a few winter vacations, though, including one memorable one to Lake Lawn Lodge on Lake Delavan, WI, where Dad took us snowmobiling across the golf course and our room was like a chalet with a neat loft where us kids got to sleep (an exciting change from the usual circumstance of having to share a double bed and/or sleep on the floor!) But no matter where we were, or when we went, the weather never seemed to be an issue. We just adjusted our plans around it, and it usually wasn't a problem. Except for one time on the summer trip we took back to Lake Lawn Lodge.

After our great time at Lake Lawn Lodge in the winter, we always talked about how fun it would be to go back up there during the summer, since there were many different activities that could be done in the summer, like swimming and boating in the lake, playing golf (or miniature golf for us kids), and others.

So many years later, Dad decided it was time to take us back to Lake Lawn for a summer vacation. We all cheered because we remembered what a great time we had there before. So we packed up our clothes and swim suits and high expectations (and the scotch cooler, of course), and headed North.

While we knew that not everything would be the same, it being summer instead of winter, we were a little taken aback, maybe even disappointed, when we got there. Probably because we were older, the room did not seem to be as big and exciting as it was when we were little. Everything else looked different too. The ground was covered in dark green grass instead of the bright white snow. But we didn't let that get us down. We decided that we would still have fun and do the activities that we hadn't been able to do in the winter. So it wasn't very long before we decided it would be fun to rent a motor boat and go out on the lake. Lake Delavan was not a small lake, and there were many little bays and beautiful summer homes that lined the shores, so it would be fun to ride around and see them. Dad was a little surprised by the cost to rent a boat, even for just an hour. But since it was something we all wanted to do, he agreed and paid the price. As we were getting ready to go, some dark grey clouds started to appear in the sky, but the attendant assured us that it was nothing to worry about. We might get a quick shower from a passing cloud, but we would probably be able to see and avoid them, or in worst case would be dry in no time riding around on the lake. So off we went. Dad was driving the boat like a seasoned Captain of the high seas, with Mom at his side. We three kids were riding on the seats in the back with the wind blowing our hair. We were having a great time, bumping up and down on the waves as we sped around admiring the scenery and homes along the shore. It wasn't more than 15 minutes, however, before the dark cloud above us opened up and started raining on us. Dad told us not to worry, we would be out of it shortly. But as we rode on, the dark cloud and rain just seemed to follow us, with the weather getting darker and colder and we got wetter and wetter. We kids were tired very quickly of being cold and wet and told Dad that we were ready to go back. But

Dad said no, he had paid for an hour, so we were going to stay out there and get his money's worth! So we kept on going farther and farther away from the Lodge, and the black cloud kept up with us all the way. Finally Dad figured it was time to turn around and head back. So he started following the opposite shore, so we could see some different houses and scenery. But all we saw was the grey wet rain and angry black waves pounding against the boat as we headed into the wind. Minutes dragged by and we got colder and wetter as we huddled under beach towels in the back of the boat, trying vainly to stay dry. After what seemed forever, the rain started letting up and the sky got a little brighter and the waves a little smoother. Finally, by the time we got back to the dock, the rain had stopped completely, and the sky was back to a clear blue again. As we walked back up the dock, shivering and dripping wet from our heads to our toes, people stopped and stared and pointed at us, talking about how we must have fallen in or capsized our boat! When we told them no, we had just been rained on, they were all astonished and couldn't believe it, as it hadn't rained at all at the Lodge. We could only shake our heads and stare off in the distance as the black cloud slowly disappeared over the horizon.

"Grand Entrance"

The summer of 1982 was an exciting time for Paul. In a year, he would be going off to college and he was looking forward to going away to school and getting out on his own. The only problem was that he didn't know where he wanted to go. He had gotten several brochures from various colleges, both local and in other states. He knew he was interested in engineering or electronics, after successfully completing a couple of electronics classes in high school - successful in that nothing melted or blew up! Plus he enjoyed putting together electronic projects and seeing them work when they were done, including a digital count down timer that was used as the electronic ignition for his model rockets. So after having browsed through many college brochures, he had narrowed it down to a few. Dad was rooting for the Air Force Academy, because it was a free college education! Paul was looking at some other colleges and universities as well, including Georgia Tech, Iowa State, and a tiny little engineering college with an unusual name, Rose-Hulman Institute of Technology, which had a funny looking college brochure with tinker toys on the cover. In order to make a final decision, Mom and Dad agreed that we should visit the most promising colleges to see first-hand some of those features that just don't come out in the brochure. The first place that we visited was the Air Force Academy in Colorado Springs, Colorado. Besides the attractive cost, the school was also in a great location, as Paul and everyone else in the family really enjoyed the mountains. The trip to the Academy was not only a school visit, but a great mini-vacation as well. Before stopping at the Academy, the family wagon made stops at the Garden of the Gods and the Royal Gorge for the typical photo opportunity. At Royal Gorge, we all walked across the suspension bridge, staring all the way down to the river, far below. Then we all took the cable car down to the bottom of the Gorge, where we walked along side the river and looked up at the tiny bridge far above. Then it was off to see the Academy. One of its most dramatic symbols is the chapel, with its multitude of spires rising into the blue sky like mountain peaks. Tall, narrow sections of beautiful stained glass windows link these spires. It certainly is an inspiring sight. But something else was what probably made the decision for Paul. As we walked out of the chapel and onto an area that overlooked the school commons, the Air Force cadets were all lining up in formations on the parade ground. We all stopped to watch. After forming up into large squadrons, the cadets precisely marched off into one of the large buildings, one group at a time. After watching this grand spectacle, we asked someone standing nearby what it represented. The answer was that the cadets were going to lunch. That reminded us that we were a little hungry as well. During the family lunch, which was a lot more chaotic than the cadet lunch by far, Mom and Dad asked

Paul if he wanted to go see more of the school or talk to the professors. Paul admitted that no, he didn't think he needed to see any more, and that maybe the Academy was not the place he wanted to go to school. The idea of having to line up and march to classes and meals and everywhere else for four years did not really appeal to him. So that eliminated the Academy, and left the decision of where to go to school still open.

The second school that was selected for a visit was Rose-Hulman Institute of Technology. This was the school whose brochure had the tinker toys prominently displayed on its cover and who claimed to be for "those who take their tinker toys seriously". It was filled with important facts about the school, including a faculty where 85% of the professors had their Masters degree, 75% of the professors had their Doctoral degree, and 50% of the professors took a bath regularly. With a student population of only 1300 undergraduates, they either were supremely selective and confident in their academic curriculum, or were a joke. So the family drove out to Terre Haute, Indiana, to find out. Winding through the streets of Terre Haute, following the vague directions (go down main street - called "Wabash Avenue" - until you see the cow pastures, then turn left), everyone was eagerly looking forward to seeing what this school was all about. As the wagon came up a hill, Mom exclaimed "Oh, I see it!" and eagerly pointed at a large, impressive looking stone archway complete with medieval stone tower standing guard over a long, tree-lined driveway. Unfortunately, that proved to be the entrance to the Highland Lawn cemetery! Everyone got a great laugh out of that, including telling the usual jokes about people dying to get in! In the end, though, they found the school just down the road, and after an enjoyable visit there, Paul decided that it was the place for him. From then on, whenever we drove past the Highland Lawn cemetery, we always remembered and teased Mom about the school's "grand entrance!"

Wild Wild West

"Ooo, Ahh, Ohh!"

As kids, we always had fun and enjoyed the many places we saw on our family vacations. But our level of enthusiasm often varied, especially on long trips, or after a long day's drive, or after visiting the umpteenth museum in a row. We tried and were usually successful at enjoying the places we visited. But not always. One of the places we drove through on our western trip in 1981 was Rocky Mountain National Park. It truly is one of the most scenic parks in America, with towering mountain peaks, quiet serene alpine lakes surrounded by beautiful meadows of wild flowers, and clear, cold mountain streams rushing and tumbling down the narrow rocky gorges. By the time we got to RMNP, though, it had been a long trip already. We had started with a train ride with Nanny across Canada from Manitoba to Vancouver where our parents picked us up. We all then drove down through Washington, Oregon, Nevada, and Utah, and were now driving across Colorado. So while the park was certainly beautiful, we had already seen a lot of mountains, including the grandeur of the Canadian Rockies. But Dad, as usual, was enjoying the views, and was talking about and pointing out the many interesting sights. Unfortunately, nobody was listening. Mom was in the front seat, working on a needlepoint piece. That was her method of passing the many hours we spent driving on any of our trips. She often completed an entire large, difficult piece in a single trip and sometimes more than one. Paul and Katie were in the back seat reading books. Paul was into mysteries, adventure, and science fiction. Katie was into romance and other teenage girl stories. Nanny was in the seat next to them, absent mindedly watching and dozing as the miles went along. Mark was tucked in the back of the white Pontiac station wagon, surrounded by suitcases and coolers, playing travel games. After a little while of being the tour guide to a group that was not very attentive, Dad finally had enough. "Hey, how about a few oo's and ahh's back there!?" Of course, we all recognized that tone of voice, when Dad was getting irritated. So we immediately put down our books and games and started watching out the windows. Then Paul said "Ooo, ahh" at something out the window. Katie and Mark immediately picked up on it, and the next thing Dad knew, Paul would start with "Ooo", Katie would reply "ahh", and Mark would finish with "ohh"! Pretty soon it was a new game, as one kid would spy something and start the "Ooo" routine, and the others would finish with the "ahh" and "ohh". It didn't take long before Dad probably regretted what he started, but as Mom reminded him, "You wanted some 'Oos' and 'ahhs', and you got them!" Later when we went on trips, if someone pointed out something they saw, the immediate response was always "Ooo", "ahh", "ohh", and then everyone in the car would burst out laughing.

"Guardrails"

Traveling with Nanny was always an adventure, and usually made a good story. Our trip out west in 1981 was no exception. During our drive through Rocky Mountain National Park, the road wound around the sides of the mountains, offering spectacular views. It was especially breathtaking when the side of the mountain gently sloped down from the road, offering a clear view of the valley below. Of course, where the side of the mountain dropped precipitously, there was usually a guardrail or stone wall to keep the cars on the road. We all enjoyed the scenery, especially Nanny. She enjoyed watching the beautiful mountains and meadows that we passed, though it was a little hard for her because, like us kids, she was not very tall, so she didn't sit very high in the seat. On several occasions, when we were pointing out interesting sights, Nanny would be sitting in the back seat saying "Where? I can't see that", and "this darn guardrail is in my way". Over and over again her view was blocked and she got frustrated with not being able to see what we were driving past. Later, as we got up to higher altitude, the area opened up and there weren't as many guardrails. About that time, Dad drove around a sharp bend that didn't have a guardrail, where the ground fell away from the road a little bit steeper than before, and we were looking out over a deep valley. At that point, Nanny, who was on the right side of the car, closest to the side of the road, shrank back a little bit in her seat and said, "whoa, that was close. They need to have a guardrail up here," at which point the rest of us burst out laughing.

"How's the Water?"

Whenever we traveled, we always liked to swim in the hotel pools where we stayed. Usually, it was the kids who were most interested in swimming, but occasionally Dad liked to take a dip as well. One of the first things we did when we got to a hotel was announce, "We're going exploring" which usually received the retort of "Find the ice machine" or even "Bring back some ice." Of course the real reason we were exploring was to find out where the pool was. Once the target had been spotted, we had to check and see how warm the water was. Even as children, with as many hotels and different places as we had stayed, we had quickly learned that not all hotel pools were created equal, or equally heated. So the first order of business when arriving was to check out the pool. Usually one or more of us would stick our hand or foot in the water to see how it felt. Then the rest of us would ask "How's the water?"

The answer would not be used to determine *whether* we would go swimming or not, merely how fast we would get ready to go swimming. You see, as kids on a family road trip, swimming was one of our greatest joys and best outlets of all. Put one of those Wal-Mart kiddie pools in front of us after driving 12 hours and we would have jumped in with smiles on. Dad, on the other hand, liked to know the answer because that *would* determine whether he went swimming or not. Since our perception of what was an acceptable temperature was usually different from Dad's, he usually ended up checking the water for himself.

But on Mark and Paul's trip out west with Dad in 1987, he took it a step further. We were on "The Boys" trip, just the three of us; out to do some sightseeing and photographing of all the smaller national parks Dad had not seen yet. Dad and Paul drove out from Iowa and picked up Mark from San Isabel Scout Ranch in Southern Colorado, where he had worked as a lifeguard for the summer. From there we proceeded on a leisurely drive through Arizona, Colorado and New Mexico to see the various sights. Arches National Park, Bryce Canyon and the "Four Corners" area were all part of our plan. One evening we stopped at a small hotel somewhere in the middle of Arizona for the night. Being in the desert in late summer, it was still fairly hot, and even though we were no longer small children who would swim in anything, the outdoor pool looked quiet, cool and inviting. Mark had already tested the water and determined that it was just right for a swim. But, as usual, Dad had to check for himself. Still wearing his shirt, shorts, and topsiders that he had been driving in, Dad wandered over to test the water. He stood at the side of the pool, hands on his hips, slipped off one shoe, and stuck his foot over the edge and gingerly into the water. However, the water level was much lower than he expected, so he kept reaching farther and farther down with his foot. What happened next left Paul and Mark rolling on the ground laughing hysterically. From our point of view, it looked like Dad just leaned over sideways, hands still on his hips, and fell into the water, like a sideways "Nestea Plunge"! While other people may have wondered or chuckled over what happened, we were laughing so hard we cried. Of course, being the affectionate and caring sons we were, our response when Dad came spluttering and splashing to the surface was, "So Dad, how's the water?"

"Rock Collecting"

Whenever we traveled, we kids always liked to bring things home as a reminder of the trip. Of course Mom and Dad did too. Like the time Mom almost drove Dad crazy because she wanted to find an eagle to take home to mount on the front of our house like the ones she saw all over New England (but that is another story.) For us kids, it was usually something smaller. In Hawaii, we collected sea shells and black sand. In New England, we found star fish and sea urchins in the tidal pools along the rocky coast (of course, we had to dry them out before we could take them home). In Texas, Paul and Mark desperately tried to catch the little chameleons that ran everywhere (and even succeeded once or twice, to Mom's consternation. Unfortunately, they usually escaped when we took them out of our styrofoam cups to look at them.)

The "Boys Trip" out west in 1987 was no different. Most of the time, our collecting centered around who could take the best picture of whatever we were looking at. (By this time, Paul and Mark were as avid photographers as Dad was. Wonder why?) Throughout all the national parks we visited, we would drive along and stop at some very scenic location (sometimes at a scenic overlook pullout, sometimes just alongside the road), jump out and take our pictures. We always kept our eyes out for something interesting to take home, usually at some corner souvenir stand. Paul had an additional incentive - his fiancée, Constance, had asked him to bring home a nice rock for her as a memento. He was continually checking out the polished rocks at all the gift shops and souvenir stands, mainly to get an idea of what to look for. He was too thrifty (or tight, as Mom would say), to actually buy a rock. He just wanted to know what kinds of rocks were in the area. By the time we were near Arches National Park, he had decided that desert sandstone would be a really neat souvenir and example of the local scenery. At one point, we had stopped somewhere at a nice, scenic location and everyone jumped out of the car to take pictures. As usual, we had all wandered off in different directions, trying to get the ultimate picture that would top everyone else's. Then as we all wandered back to the car, Mark joined up with Paul as we headed back to meet Dad, who was already waiting at the car. He never seemed to wander quite as far as we did, probably because we were usually climbing up a huge boulder, or rock-hopping out in a stream, or peering over a steep cliff. As we walked back, Paul found a rock that would be perfect to take home to give to Constance. Soon, Dad saw Paul and Mark coming back through the sage brush, walking side by side, but bent over in a funny way. "What's the matter?" came his concerned voice. "Nothing, just found a rock to take to Constance" was our reply. Dad gasped as he saw the boulder we struggled to carry back up the sandy trail. (Ok, maybe it wouldn't really be classified as a boulder, but it sure felt like it.) "Where do you think you are going to fit that in?" was his comment. As usual, the Red Wagon (our Chevy station wagon) was loaded down with suitcases and all the comforts of home. "We'll find a place" we assured him. Soon we had rearranged things in the back seat and made a place for the rock on the floor. Then we all got back in and headed on our way. Shortly, we passed an Arches National Park sign. Suddenly, Mark pointed at the sign and said "oops!" We all looked, and at the bottom of the sign, in the lists of do's and don'ts, was the statement that rock collecting was not allowed. We all looked at each other, knowing that no one would believe us if we told them we picked up the rock outside the park. (that's our story anyway, and we're sticking to it.) Mark, who was in the back seat at that time, took an old army blanket that Dad always had in the car and quickly covered up the rock. Whenever we would see a park ranger vehicle, we would all busily look everywhere but at the ranger himself. Weeks later, when Paul gave the rock to Constance, she asked where in the world we found that. "Oh, just went rock collecting" was the reply.

Southern Comfort

"Fun in the Sun"

It is every teenage kid's dream to go to Florida for spring break. We were no exception. Being from the Midwest, it was a little hard to get down to Florida, since none of us had a car of our own, and Mom and Dad weren't about to let us take theirs, or any one else's for that matter. Not that we would want to be caught dead driving the family station wagon on spring break. For many years we just dreamed about it. Then in 1983, the year Paul graduated from high school, Mom and Dad announced that we were all going to Florida during spring break. Our initial reaction was "spring break, with our parents?!" But then reality set in and we realized that it was either that, or spend that week off in cold, dreary, Newton, Iowa! Once that became clear, the decision was easy. The plans went forward to spend a week at the Five Flags Inn on Pensacola Beach for our spring vacation. We eagerly anticipated the fun and excitement we would have on the beach, with the sun and water and all the gorgeous girls in bikinis and (for Katie) the cute guys in Speedos. That was before we knew where exactly Pensacola Beach was. As it turned out, Pensacola Beach is on the panhandle of Florida, on the Gulf of Mexico. The beaches there are sparkling white, silky sand beaches, under a brilliant spring sun in the clear blue sky. A teenager's dream come true. There was only one problem. Spring in the panhandle is warm, but nowhere near the hot sunny days that most spring-breakers head for. In fact the water is downright cold, and the days can be cool enough to require wearing a jacket. As a result, there weren't that many bikinis or Speedos on the beach. But that didn't dampen our spirits. We were on the beach, in sunny Florida, on spring break! We made the most of it. In fact, the first full day we were there, as soon as we had finished eating some cereal in our rooms, we were out on the beach. And we stayed there for the rest of the day. We fed the sea gulls, looked for sea shells, played with our Frisbee and paddle ball, laid on towels in the sun, and even occasionally, when the afternoon warmed up, got into the water to splash in the waves. Mark and Paul had noticed that a few other people had made fabulous sand sculptures, so they were soon hard at work building sand castles, sports cars, sea creatures, and anything else they could think of. By the end of the day, we were all very tired and very happy. And, as we kids were soon to find out, very sunburned! While we had put sun screen on in the morning, we had forgotten to put on any more during the day. As most parents know, sun lotions are not designed to handle the sand and salt water and long hours of exposure to the direct sun with just one application. As a result, we were very red and sore by that evening. Katie fared the best, since she had spent most of the time on her beach towel, and had remembered to put lotion on more often. Even then her face was a bright, lobster red. Paul had his shirt on most of the morning, so his shoulders and back were only slightly burned, but his face had a nice bright glow to it. However, he had been barefoot all day and the tops of his feet were a deep, crimson red, causing pain just to look at them! Mark, though, had only had his swim trunks on all day, and he was dark red from head to foot. He was so burned that at night he couldn't even have a sheet covering him because it hurt too much. Mom and Dad went to the local beach shop and bought pure aloe vera gel by the gallon and slathered it liberally and frequently over everyone. That night was very uncomfortable and sleepless for most of us. The next day we spent in the car, riding around sightseeing at various places. If Paul got out, he sort of hobbled around, because his feet were so sore. Mark didn't even get out, because it was too painful to wear socks or shoes. The next day was only a little better. Again the idea of being in the sun was unthinkable, so we went shopping instead. In one particular beach store, as we were browsing around, looking at various sea shells, carved ships, and other nautical gifts, a young clerk came up to us and asked how come we were spending our day inside instead of out on the beach enjoying the sun. We all looked at her, and after seeing the color of our faces, she blinked and said "oh, I guess you already have." We just smiled and went on our way. Fortunately we did recover by the end of the week, and over all had a truly wonderful spring break. But we will always remember the time we had too much fun in the sun.

West Coast Wandering

"S'more please!"

One of the greatest things about going on our family trips when we were kids, were the snacks we invariably got to eat. At home, Mom and Dad were very strict on when we could have snacks, and it was very rare when we got to eat anything other than crackers or maybe some fruit. But on trips it was a different story. We always had some chips or candy bars in the car on the long days when we would be traveling 400 - 500 miles or more. When we got to the hotel after a long drive, we always got to have some snacks with soda while Mom and Dad had their snacks and "drinks" out of the old, scotch plaid cooler that went on every trip. In addition, on days that we spent our time at the pool while Dad was in his business meetings, Mom would always fill her bag with snacks to munch on throughout the day. It was no different during our trip out west in 1981. Dad and Mom had picked all three of us kids up in Vancouver, British Columbia, after our train ride across Canada with Nanny. From there we drove down the coast of Washington, and stopped for a few days in Newport, Oregon. Dad had gotten us a really neat hotel right on Agate Beach. (As we said, a "neat" hotel to us meant that it either had a pool or a beach, and preferably both!) We spent our days playing on the beach, looking for agates, or sightseeing, such as at nearby Yaquina Head lighthouse. As usual, snacks were available throughout the day. But on that trip, we got to have an extra special treat. We must have been in a small supermarket when one of us kids saw marshmallows and that triggered a thought. "Can we have s'mores, Mom?" We had been in girl and boy scouts long enough to learn what s'mores were, and how good they were. But Nanny didn't know what we were talking about. "What are s'mores?" We had to explain how to melt the marshmallows and put them on chocolate bars and graham crackers. That sounded interesting to Nanny, so that settled it. Mom bought the necessary supplies, and we were all set. Except for one small problem. There were no cooking facilities in our hotel room. After consulting with Dad, it was decided that we could have a cookout on the beach and make s'mores. Dad got the stuff necessary to have our cookout. The weather on the day we had picked for the cookout, though, was cloudy, windy and cool. But that did not dampen our enthusiasm. That evening after dinner we bundled up in our jackets, took our bag of marshmallows, chocolate bars, and crackers and headed down to the beach. Nanny was especially concerned about the weather, but we assured her we would keep her warm. We found large pieces of drift wood to sit on and enough small ones for our fire. Soon we were huddled around the flames, as the sun slowly sank through the clouds and disappeared into the ocean. The wind whipped our jackets around and about us. We held onto sticks with marshmallows stuck on the end of them, roasting them and plopping them onto the waiting crackers and chocolate bars before we eagerly put them into our mouths. Even Nanny agreed that it was worth the cold and wind to have a fun cookout on the beach. Soon she was holding out her stick with the rest of us kids, asking for "s'more, please!"

"No Thank You"

Long driving trips tend to breed repetition and boredom. When you travel 500+ miles a day, or over 1000 miles in a few days, with two tired parents, two or three jumpy kids, an overly helpful grandmother, plus six or eight suitcases and several bags of food, all in a single car, no matter how large a station wagon it is, you get a little stir crazy. And when that happens, anything can happen. The slightest comment can start a heated argument, or hysterical laughter. On our second trip out west in 1985, there were several instances of each.

This trip, with Mom and Dad, Katie, Mark, and Nanny (who flew out and joined us in California; Paul was at a Scout camp in Colorado), started out as most did with long drives along the interstates. We rolled through Midwestern cornfields, western mountains, then the deserts, and finally approached the border of California. But before you get into California, you have to stop at the state line. No, you are not entering another country (at least not offically). But you are entering a prime agricultural area, and one that the California state government takes great efforts to protect from external parasites. That does not mean the tourists, who are welcomed with open arms (and hands). But fruit or plants are not. California has strict rules about bringing in produce and plants of any kind from outside the state. They have set up agricultural inspection stations at all the major interstate border crossings. Usually for tourists entering the state, these are simple formalities, since most of them don't travel with their houseplants or garden produce. But for the Siebels (aka the Midwestern Griswalds), nothing is simple or straightforward.

As the Siebels' Red Wagon approached the border, there were several cars in line waiting to go through the inspection station. Dad got in line with all the others, with Mom, Mark and Katie more or less ignoring everything around them because they were engrossed in needlepoint or books or sleeping. As they drew closer to the agricultural inspector, Dad rolled down his window to get ready to talk to him. We couldn't help but overhear the conversation with the preceding cars. As a car drew up, the inspector said "Good Morning. Do you have any plants or fruits?" The travelers usually responded with a "no." Then the inspector would say "Have a nice day" as he opened the barrier. The travelers usually replied "thank you" as they drove on through. Two cars ahead of us, the same routine: "Good Morning. Do you have any plants or fruits?" "No." "Have a nice day." "Thank you." Then again for the car ahead of us: "Good Morning. Do you have any plants or fruits?" "No." "Have a nice day." "Thank you." Finally it was our turn. Dad drove up and smiled at the inspector who started his routine: "Good Morning. Do you have any plants or fruits?" All the repetition must have gotten to Dad. Without giving it a thought, he simply replied "No, thank you." The inspector was caught off guard and stood there speechless, probably wondering what Dad was trying to say. Of course, the long hours of driving had affected everyone else in the car as well, because instantly we all broke out laughing. Since the inspector couldn't figure out whether Dad was trying to say he didn't have any plants or fruits, or didn't want any plants or fruits, he simply opened the barrier without another word. Dad just smiled as he drove through, with the rest of us still laughing hysterically in the background.

"Picnic in the Park"

It's no surprise that families are a cause of great embarrassment among teenagers. We kids suffered through much of it growing up, although no more than any other "normal" family. On family vacations, when you can't escape your family, it is a prime time for embarrassing moments. Katie's "most embarrassing moment" happened in California in 1985 just hours before we lost the bumper (another story and cause of great embarrassment for Katie. It was not a good day). The family was driving around Monterey, admiring the beautiful scenery and taking in the sights of the town. We had recently arrived and it was too early to check into our hotel. As usual, we had everything we could possibly need in the station wagon, including leftover KFC from the night before. It was nearing lunchtime and the gang was hungry. Katie was thinking McDonald's or Wendy's would fit the bill nicely. But, either she was outvoted or Dad couldn't find a fast food restaurant. What he did find was a "park" or something he thought looked like a park, with a beautiful view overlooking the Monterey coastline. It was decided that we could eat the leftovers in the "park" and have a picnic. Katie was mortified! She was convinced that Dad's so called "park" was actually private property. It was in a residential area with a row of houses on one side of the street and this lovely expanse of green grass and trees on the other. There were no picnic tables, benches or signs to indicate this was a public park. But even as Katie protested and pointed these things out, Dad was parking the car. Fueled by her embarrassment, Katie was now furious. She was being humiliated beyond measure! There they were, tourists from Iowa, rummaging around in the back of the fully loaded station wagon, complete with luggage carrier on top, for the leftover chicken, drinks and a couple of army blankets on which to have their "picnic" in somebody's front yard! To add insult to injury, Dad insisted on commemorating the event with a picture! As if Katie had not endured enough. To this day, that is one of the most memorable, talked about pictures in the family. Everyone is enjoying the lovely picnic on the coast of California except Katie, who had daggers shooting from her eyes!!

"I Left My Bumper in Monterey"

When driving across the country and especially in California, in a weighed down, over stuffed, wood paneled station wagon with Iowa license plates, you get used to the fact that people are going to stare at you. You begin to get the feeling that you are the main attraction. It's like an Amish farmer in Pennsylvania, only we were Iowa farmers who actually ventured off the farm. In fact, many times we talked about adding a hand written sign in the rear window that said "Yes, we are from Iowa, NO, we are not farmers". So to say that we got used to it and actually had fun with it would be a reasonably accurate statement. That is, until one sunny afternoon at the Holiday Inn parking lot in Monterey, California, during our western trip in 1985.

We had spent the day, as usual, on the road packed inside the wagon like sardines in a can with little tiny windows that we could peek from. The sun was just beginning to make its final descent for the day and the afternoon had the feel of that peaceful quiet of a summer day coming to rest. We were all tired and anxious to get checked into the hotel - for Mom and Dad that meant relaxing and enjoying "tea time" and for us kids it meant cooling off in the pool. When we pulled into the parking lot all we were thinking about was getting into the hotel as fast as we could. Again the Red Wagon was so loaded down in the back that the front was pointing high into the air. Mom almost needed a step stool to get in to the front seat! When Dad failed to brake at a speed bump that he didn't see, one that had been strategically placed just to slow such people down, the back end of the car broke the afternoon silence with such a thunderous noise that people came running out of their hotel rooms as if a canon had been fired.

Now, it was not unusual for the back end of the car to scrape the ground occasionally on a Siebels' vacation, but this had such intensity it surprised us all. Mark was in the "way" back and scrambled to the rear window hoping to see a cool gouge in the semi-soft blacktop of the parking lot. What he saw was the gleaming chrome of the 6 foot wide rear bumper of the station wagon rocking back and forth in the evening sun like a shiny, abandoned, aluminum canoe stuck on a rock in the middle of a rushing river. This was not one of the new style bumpers made of a skinny steel bar wrapped in plastic; no, this was the type of bumper you could actually use to dent a brink wall. Mark jumped forward and, wanting to fully explain the situation, yelled "We lost the bumper... I mean the WHOLE bumper!"

It became even more evident that this was no wimpy bumper when Dad and Mark had to walk back and retrieve the now orphaned bumper and carry it to an empty parking spot - it was heavy and took up most of the space. By this time even more people had come out of their rooms, pointing and giggling, standing on their balconies watching the "farmers" pick up their bumper. Mom thought the whole event was too funny, and sat in the front seat laughing hysterically while Dad and Mark struggled with it. Katie, being an all American teenage girl and wearing her emotions on her sleeve, was embarrassed to her core. If she could have crawled under Mom's seat, she would have, and would have stayed there until the cover of darkness could obscure her identity. In the mean time, after getting the bumper out of the middle of the parking lot and dropping it (literally) in an empty parking spot, Dad got out his trusty screwdriver and removed the license plate. He had decided he would leave the bumper there because he figured he could get a new one when he got home (yet another story), especially since there was nowhere to put it in the overloaded car. After retrieving the license plate, he told Mark to get back into the car and Mom to stop laughing because they were leaving. After all the attention they had gotten by now, he was in no mood to go into the hotel and ask for a room! From that point on we didn't have any kind of sign or declaration in the window, just an Iowa license plate duct taped to the rear window of a bumper-less, wood paneled, station wagon. Tony Bennett may have left his heart in San Francisco, but the Siebels left their bumper, not to mention their self respect, in Monterey.

"Whoop Whoops"

Southern California is known for sun, sand, movie stars and earthquakes. During our trip there in the summer of '85, we spent plenty of time in the sun and sand, but we missed the movie stars. We did not, however, miss the earthquakes.

We were in San Diego at the beautiful Hotel Del Coronado for one of Dad's Maytag meetings. San Diego is also home to the North Island Naval Air Station and we would often see, and hear, the military planes flying low, just offshore, on their practice flights. The base was practically within spitting distance from the hotel. There was a certain kind of plane that would make a bizarre "whoop, whoop" kind of noise as it went by. Dad said it had to do with the wings changing formation as it came in to land. Anyway, Mom started calling those planes the "whoop, whoops" since they were very loud and you could hear them over everything else. As was often the case, Mom and Dad had some special dinner they had to attend one night. Mom was in the bathroom getting ready and the rest of us were watching TV while Dad enjoyed a before-dinner cocktail. All of a sudden, the room started shaking. Not violently, but enough that you could see and feel everything in the room vibrating with motion. Wide-eyed, Dad, Katie and Mark just looked at each other. Then Mom piped up from the bathroom, "My, that was a big whoop, whoop!" And we all yelled in unison, "That wasn't a whoop, whoop! That was an earthquake!", much to Mom's astonishment. Later, we verified it on the news and we actually experienced a few more tremors that evening after our parents went out. To a couple of kids who grew up in the Midwest, we were familiar with severe thunderstorms and even tornados and knew what to do in case of those emergencies. But, as one particular tremor seemed to last forever, Mark and Katie just looked at each other, at a loss for what to do. Finally, Mark exclaimed, "If it doesn't stop soon, I'm going to jump off the balcony!" (We were on the second floor). Luckily, there was no damage and no immediate danger. It did, however, make for a very memorable trip! And from then on, whenever there was a loud noise, we always said, "there goes Mom's whoop whoops!"

"Hotel Hazards"

As we've said before, when the Siebels traveled, we packed everything so that there was nothing left to chance, including the proverbial "kitchen sink". In addition, when Nanny traveled with us, we always got two rooms, one for our parents and one for her. Katie usually stayed in the room with Nanny and the boys with Mom and Dad. Nanny always came well prepared, too. For example, she had this nifty little device, a heating coil, which would boil a cup of water for coffee or tea. In those days, they didn't have coffee makers in all the hotel rooms, so it was nice to be able to make a cup of coffee without leaving your room. To use it, you placed it in a cup (not plastic) with water, and then plugged it into the wall. It would heat the water, very quickly, to boiling. For safety reasons you always put it into the liquid before plugging it in.

On our trip out west in 1985, after we picked up Nanny at the airport, we stayed in a Hilton in the Los Angeles area. We had spent a couple of days there going to Universal Studios, the Queen Mary II, and the Spruce Goose to name a few of the many attractions. On the day we were to leave, Nanny was up fairly early to get packed. Katie, staying in her room and being the teenager that she was, was desperately trying to sleep in. She was trying to ignore Nanny who was puttering around the room. With one eye open, she noticed Nanny walk over to the little table beside the bed. She saw Nanny lean down, and then turn around to head back to the bathroom. Katie squeezed her eyes shut willing herself back to sleep, when something made her take another look. At first she couldn't believe it, but as she sat up, there was no mistaking the smoke and flames as a little fire took shape on the carpet where Nanny had laid the heating coil! Frozen in place, Katie shrieked, "Nanny!" Our little grandmother, dressed in her robe and satin slippers came running across the room mumbling "Oh, horrors!" and stomped on the flame until it was extinguished. Katie, meanwhile, after the shock had worn off, rolled on the bed, howling with laughter! She had never seen her grandmother move so fast! Nanny never could explain what had possessed her to plug in the heating coil and leave it on the carpet. The little fire had left quite a burnt spot in the carpet, and Nanny debated about whether she should notify the hotel office. In the end, she simply placed one of the room chairs strategically over the burn, and left it at that. All of us were quite shocked at Nanny's subterfuge, but as we drove away she made the remark, "That hotel was overpriced, anyway!"

About the Authors

Paul has spent 19 years in the US Air Force as an engineer. He and his wife, Constance, and daughter, Olivia, have lived all over the US as well as Europe. They enjoy traveling, camping, photography, and pets, of which they currently have three cats: Sebastian, Samson and Panda Bear, and a very spoiled Cavalier King Charles Spaniel puppy named Lacy Valentine. They currently live in southern California.

Katie is a graphics designer (whose work includes the front and back covers of this book.) She and her husband, Drake, and son, Jonathan, enjoy traveling, photography and kicking back in the sun and sand. They have a very spoiled 18 pound black cat named Shadow. They currently live in northern Virginia.

Mark is supervisor of risk analysis for a higher education services company. He and his wife Christina have three daughters: Nicole, Rachael, and Riley who participate in soccer, karate, and drama. They love swimming, camping, and most recently, boys. As a family they also enjoy traveling, camping, photography, and partying with friends. They have an assortment of pets that include 4 cats: Spike, Sky, Hershey, and Popcorn, and an 80 pound Rhodesian Ridgeback, named Kutcher. They currently lease space from their pets in the Denver Colorado area.

www.ingramcontent.com/pod-product-compliance
Lightning Source LLC
Chambersburg PA
CBHW030029290326
41934CB00005B/554